MY first toddler COLORinG BOOK

nuMBeRS

ONE

TWO

THREE

FOUR

FIVE

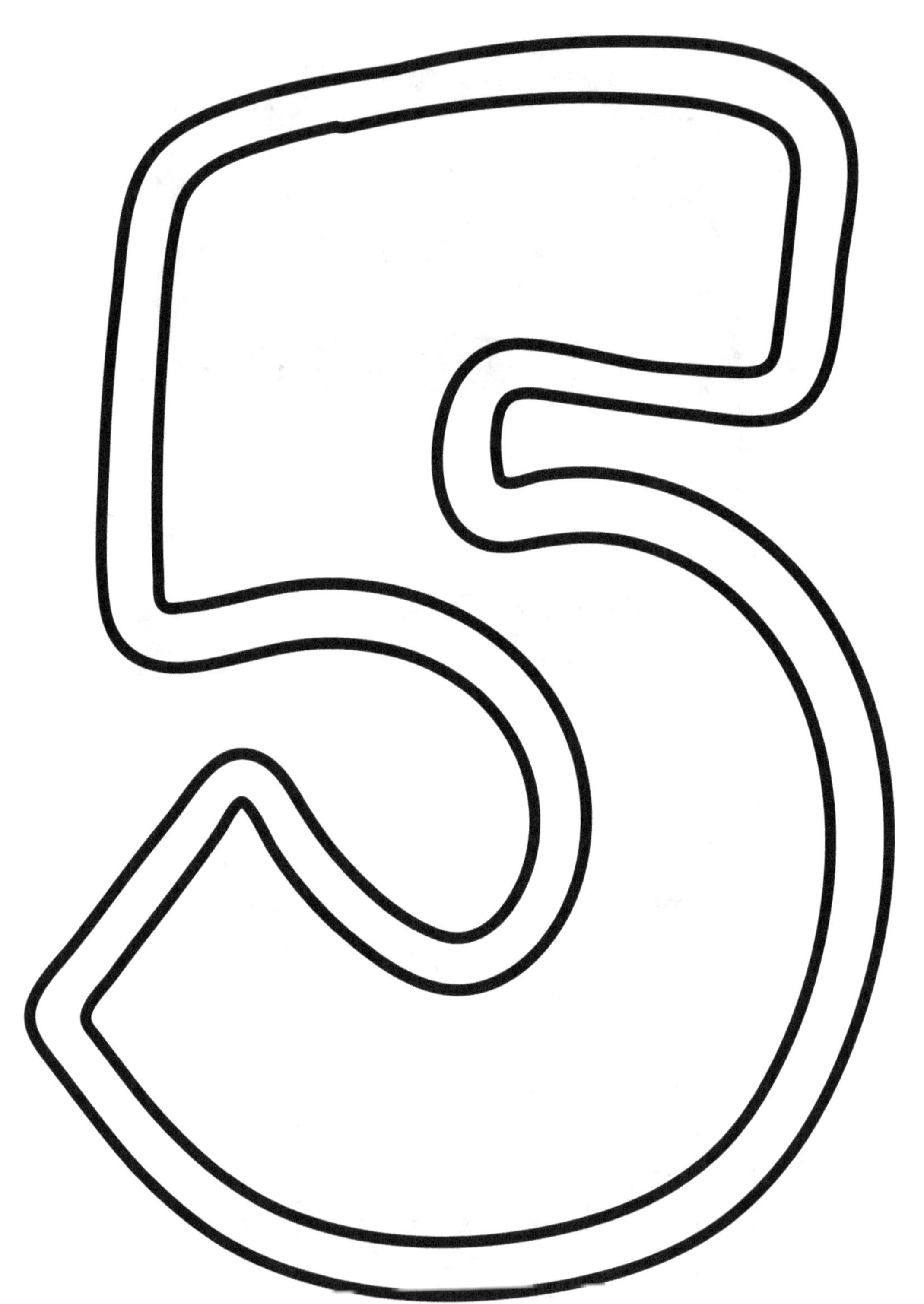

SIX

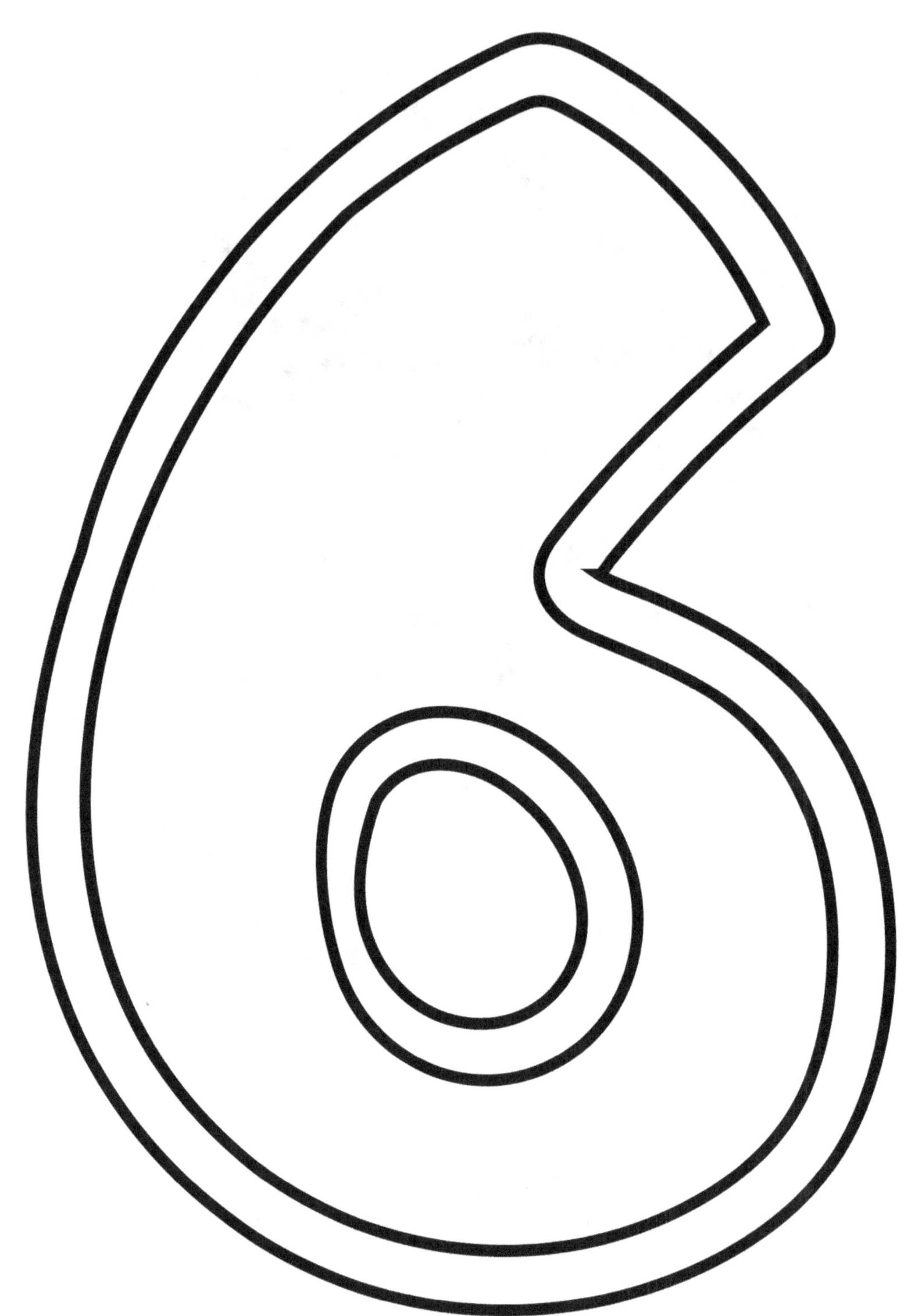

SEVEN

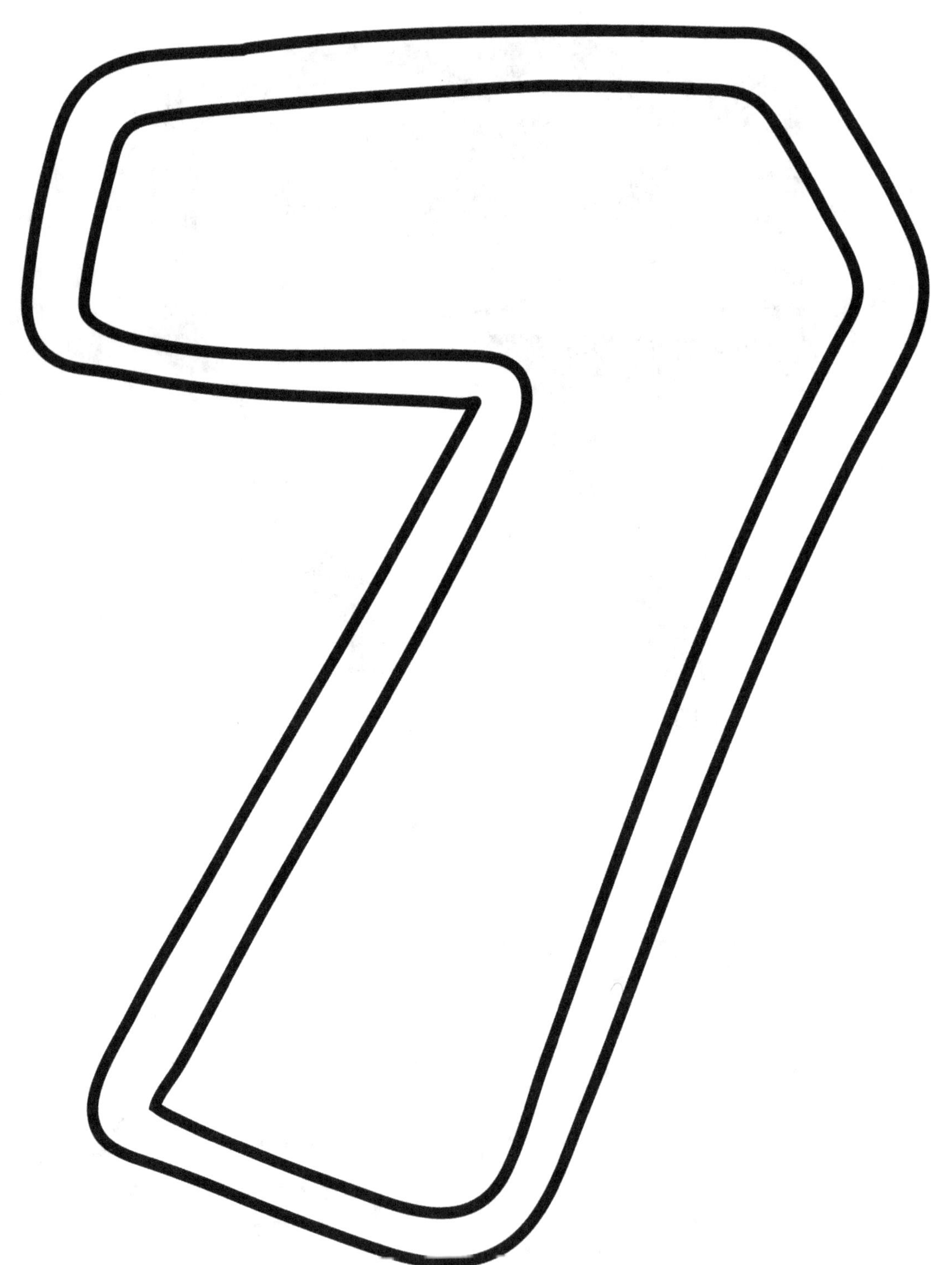

EIGHT

NINE

TEN

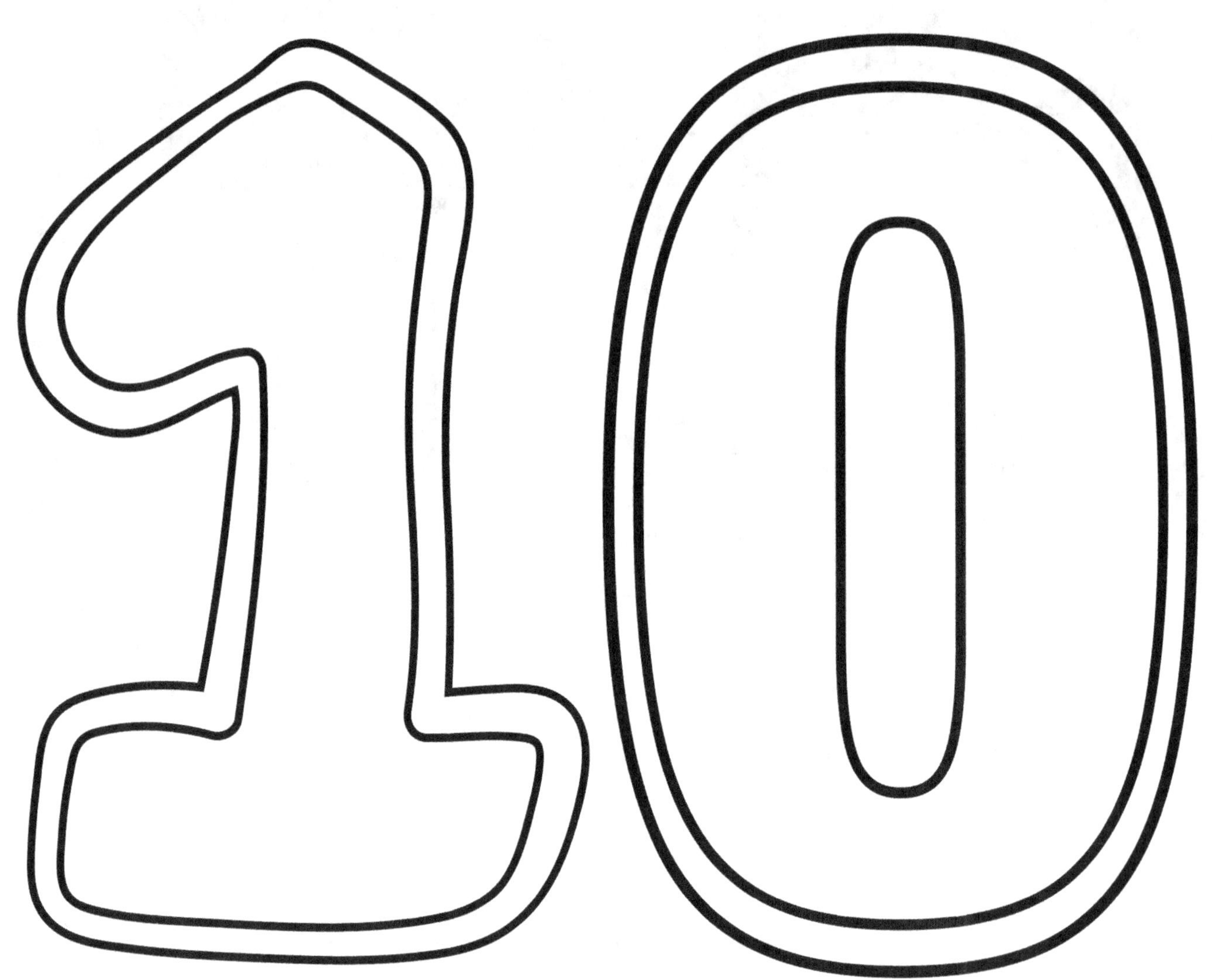

Letters and Animals

A
alligator

A
alligator

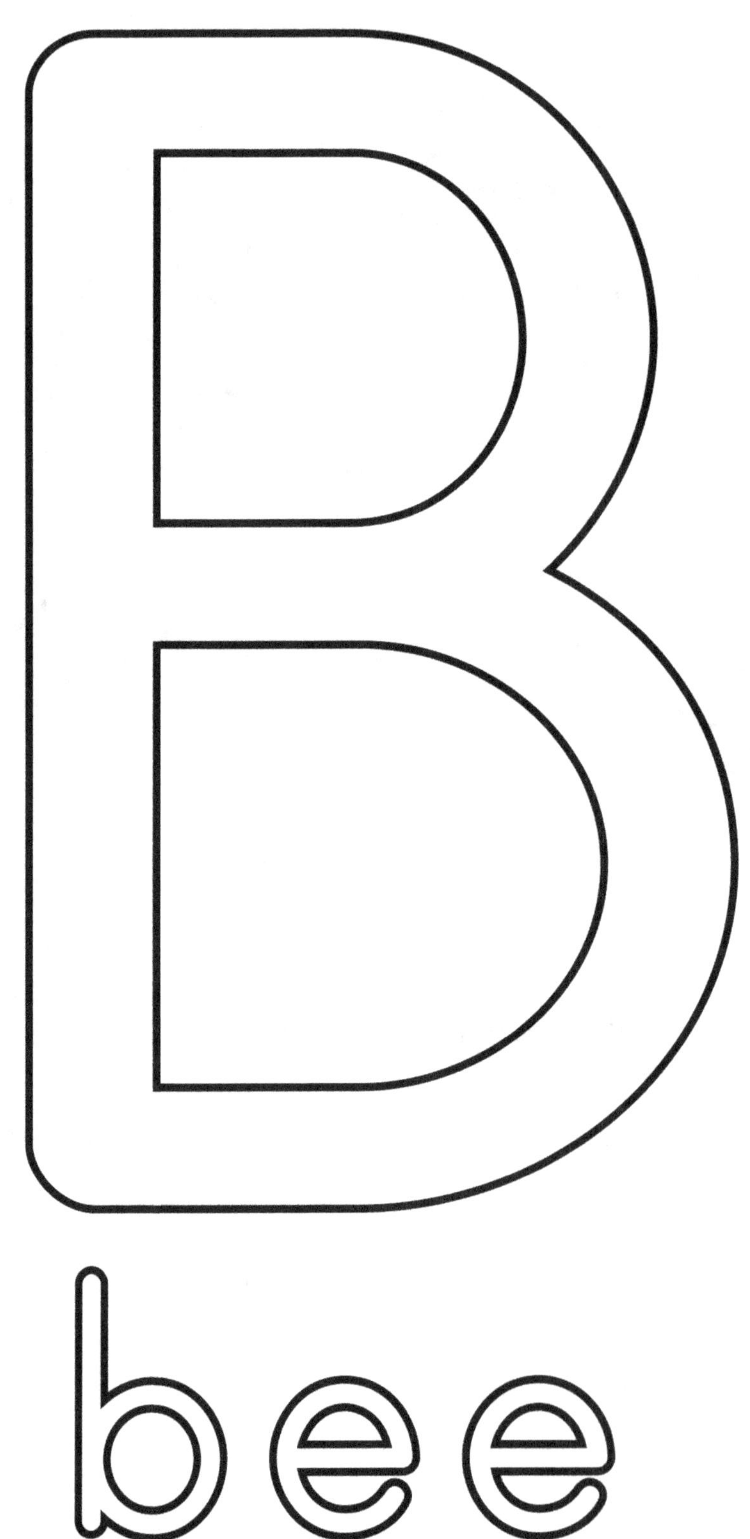

B
bee

bee

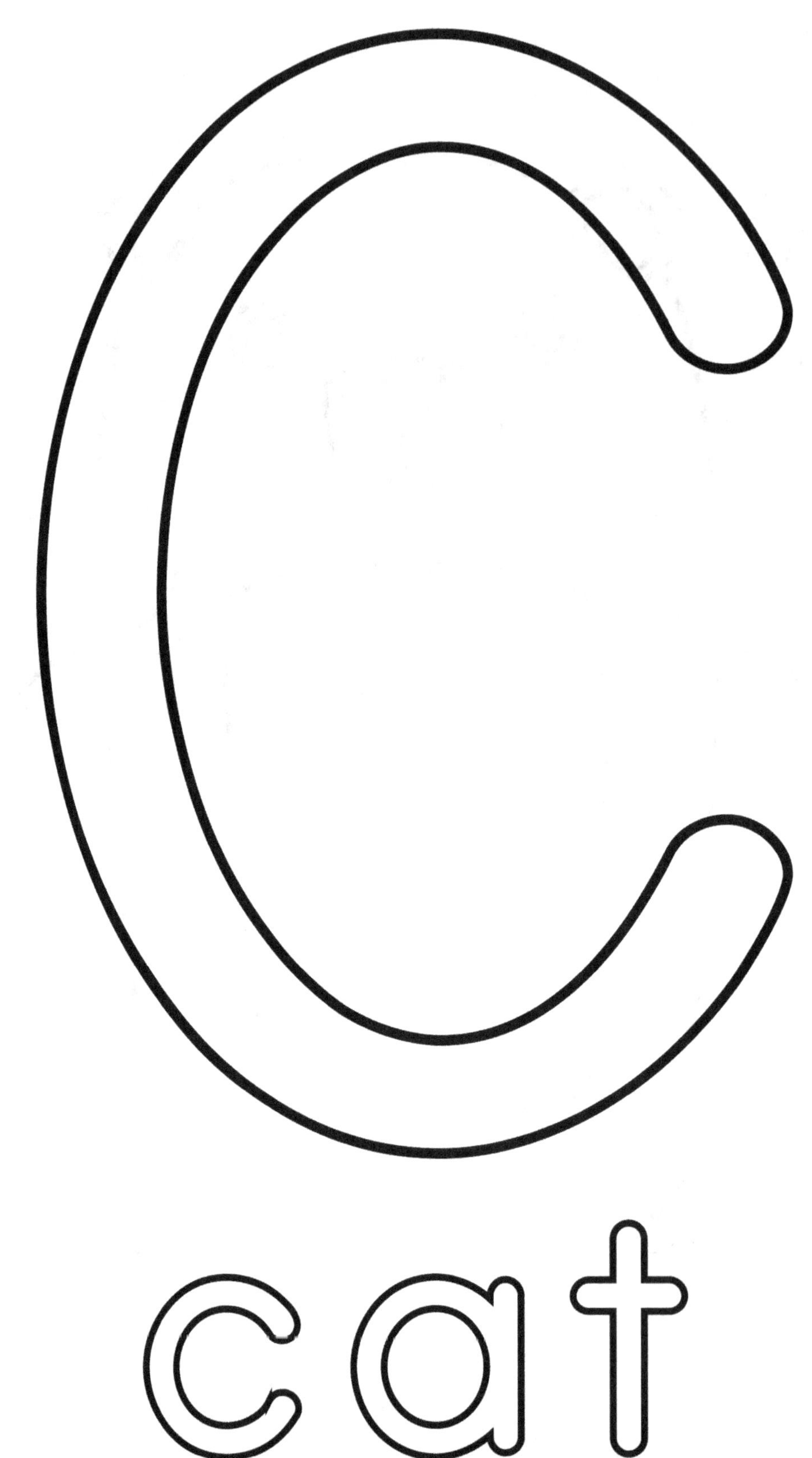

cat

C
cat

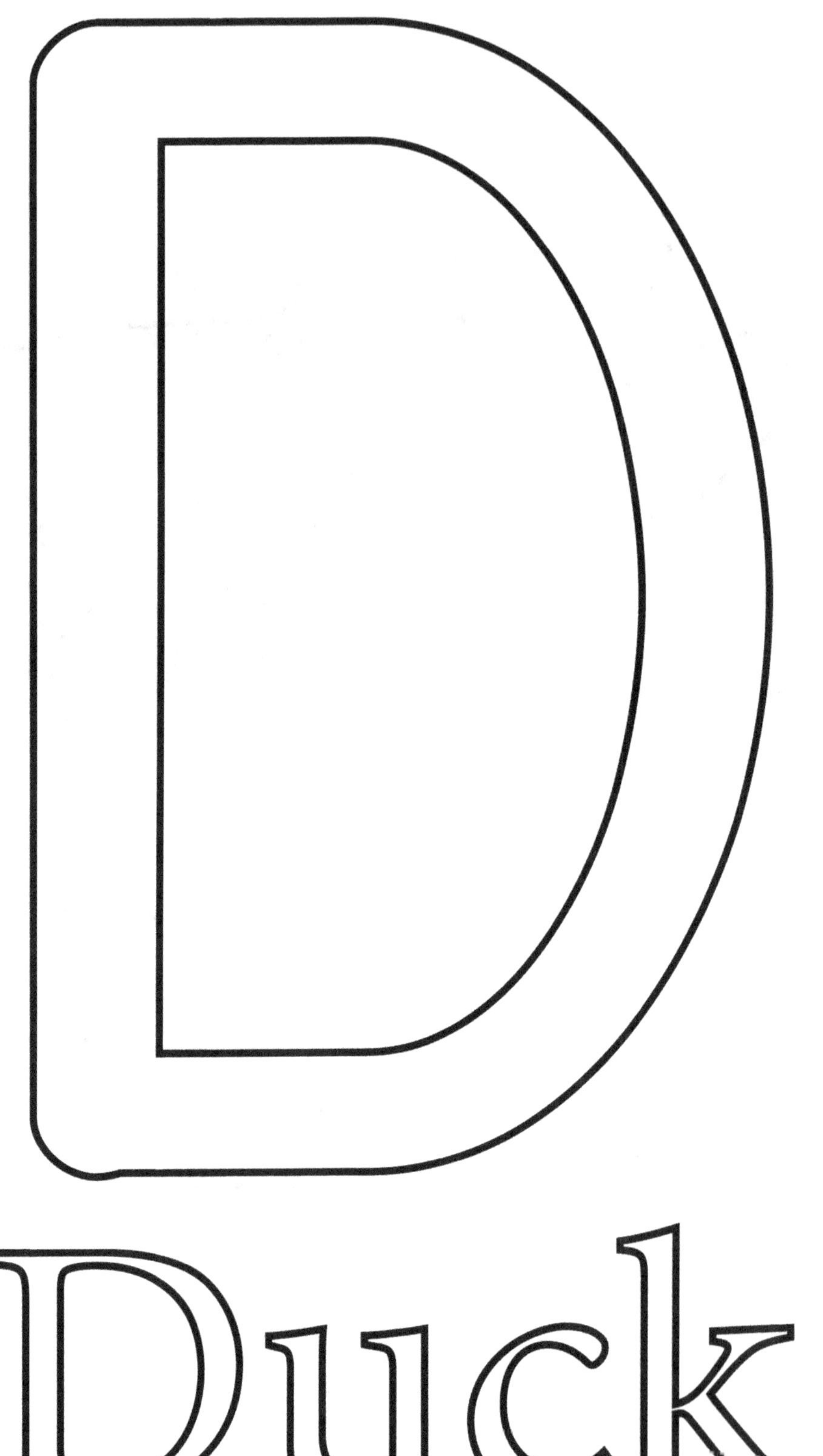

D
Duck

D

Duck

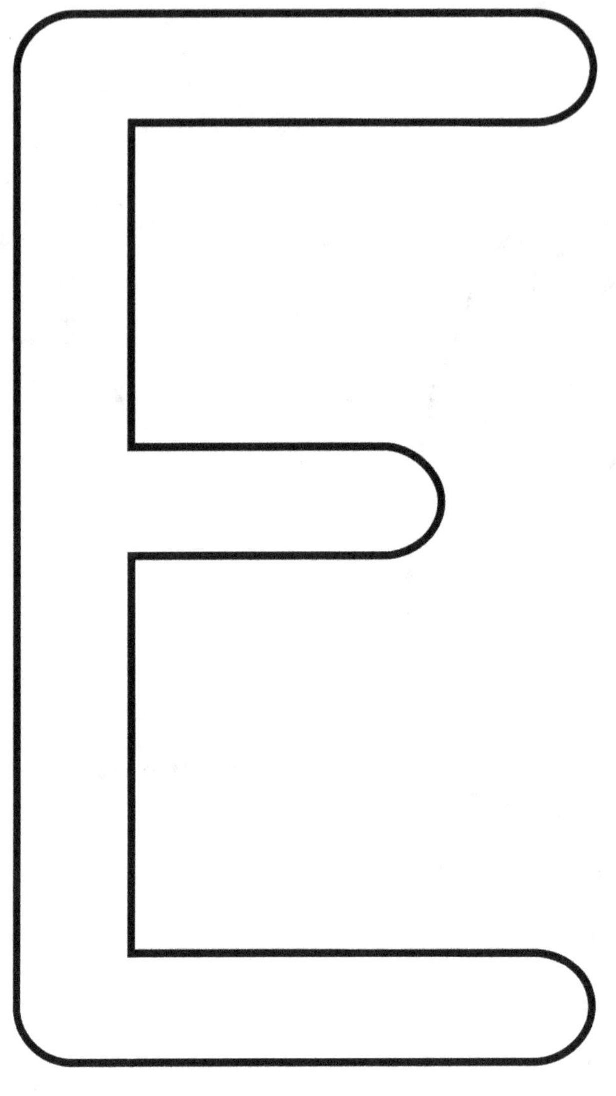

elephant

E

elephant

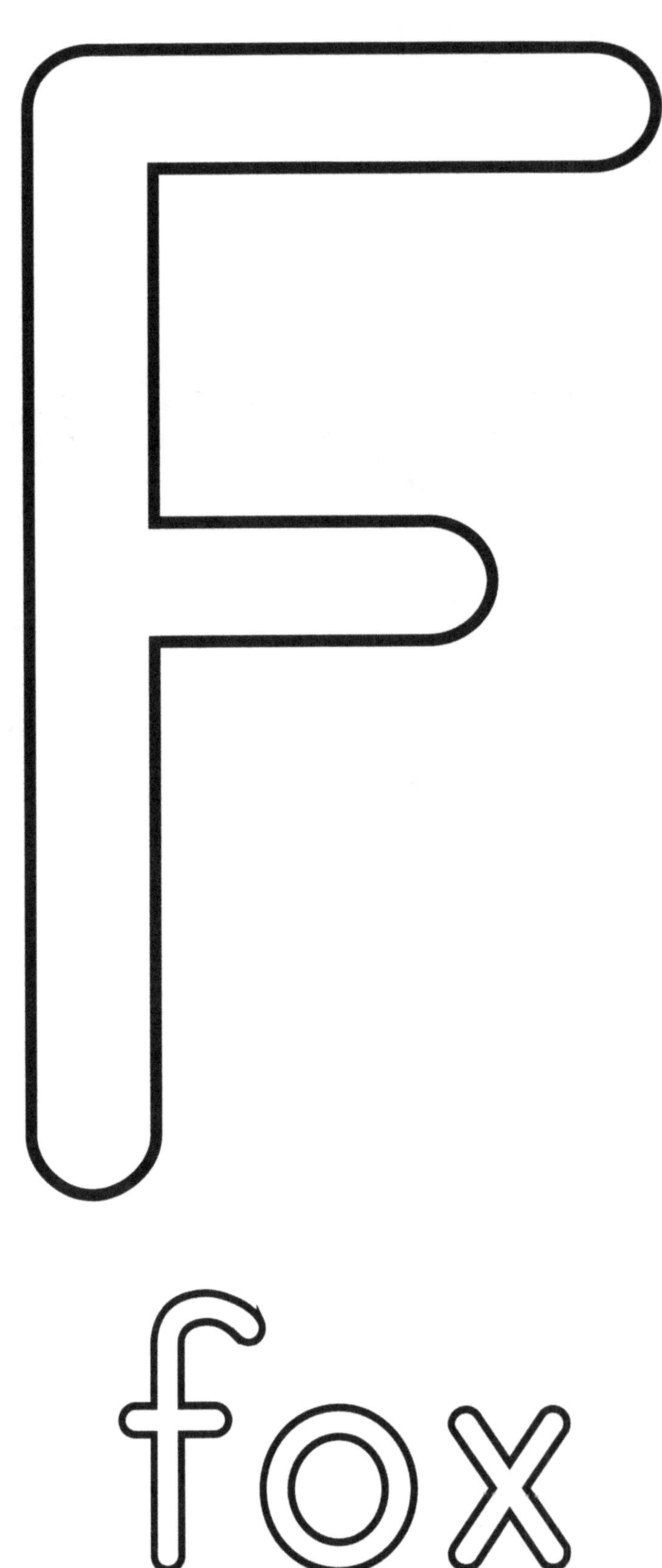

fox

F

fox

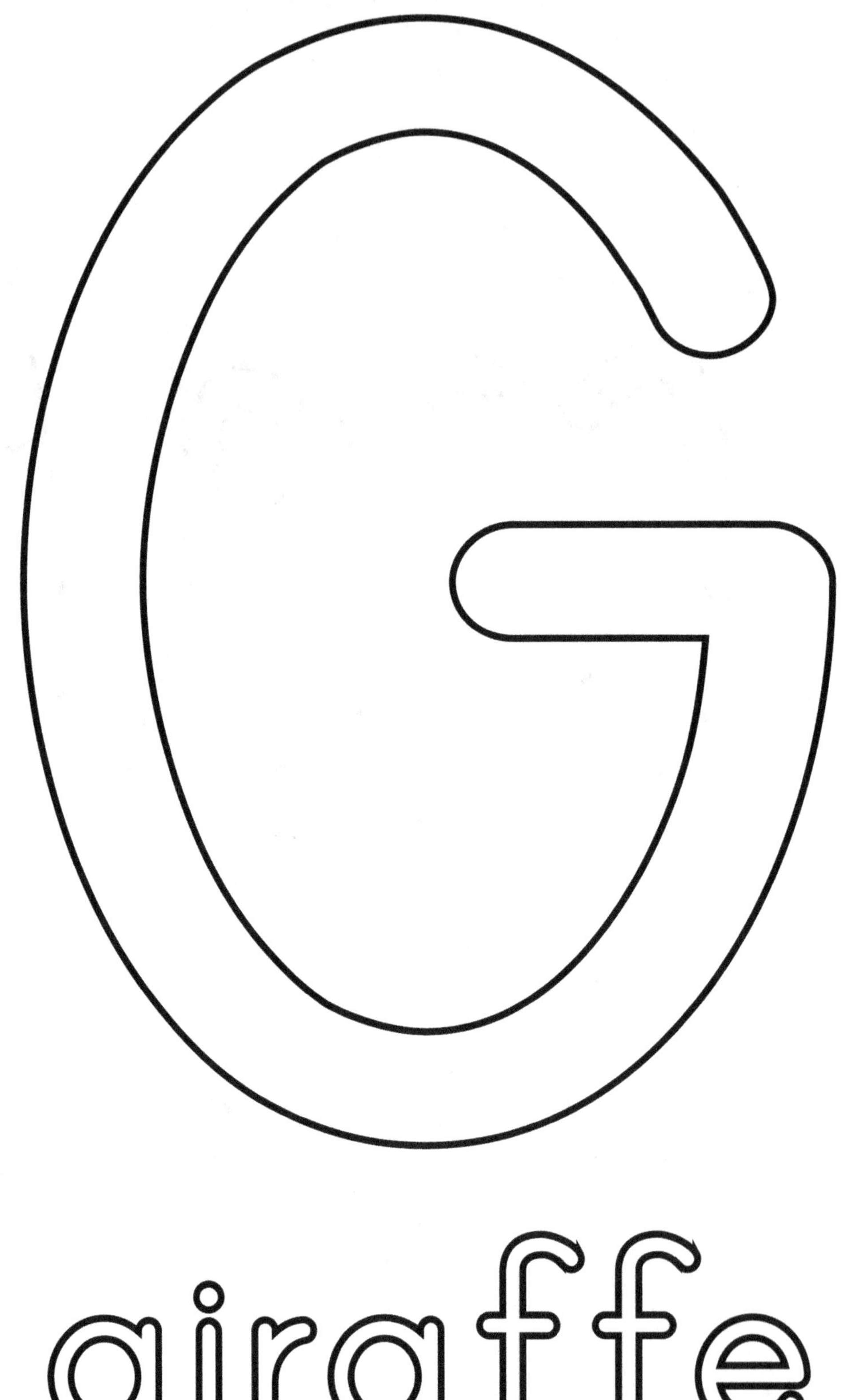

giraffe

giraffe

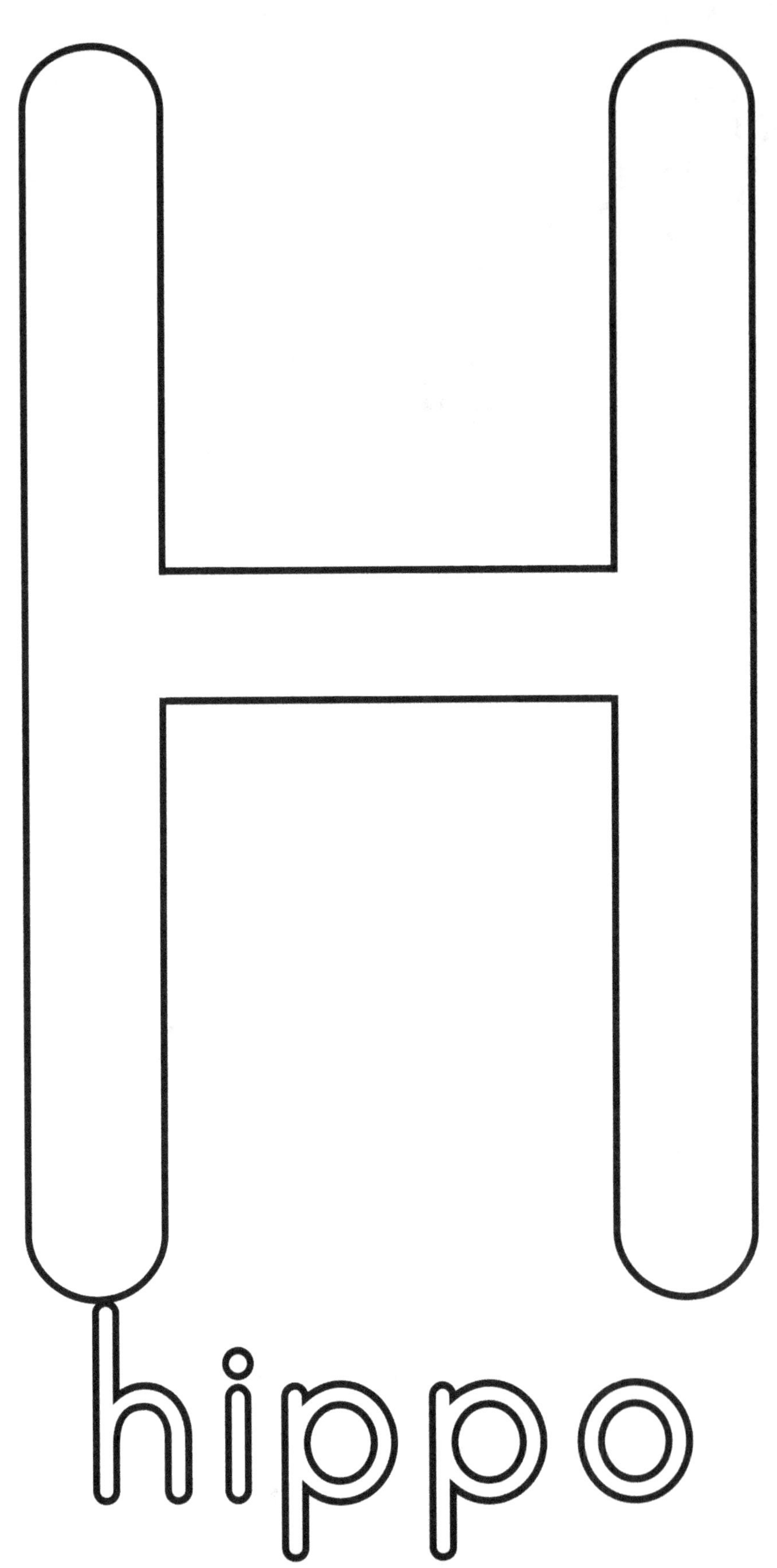
hippo

H

hippo

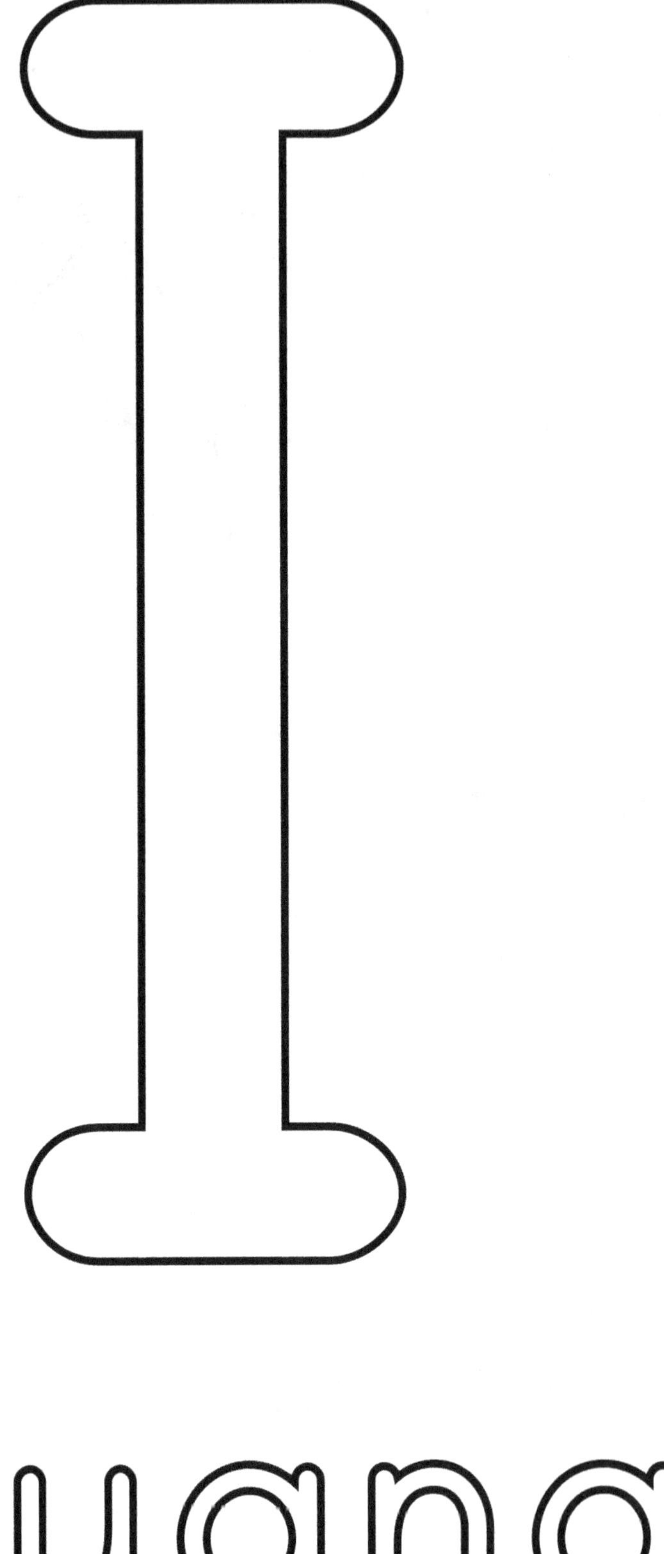

I

iguana

I

iguana

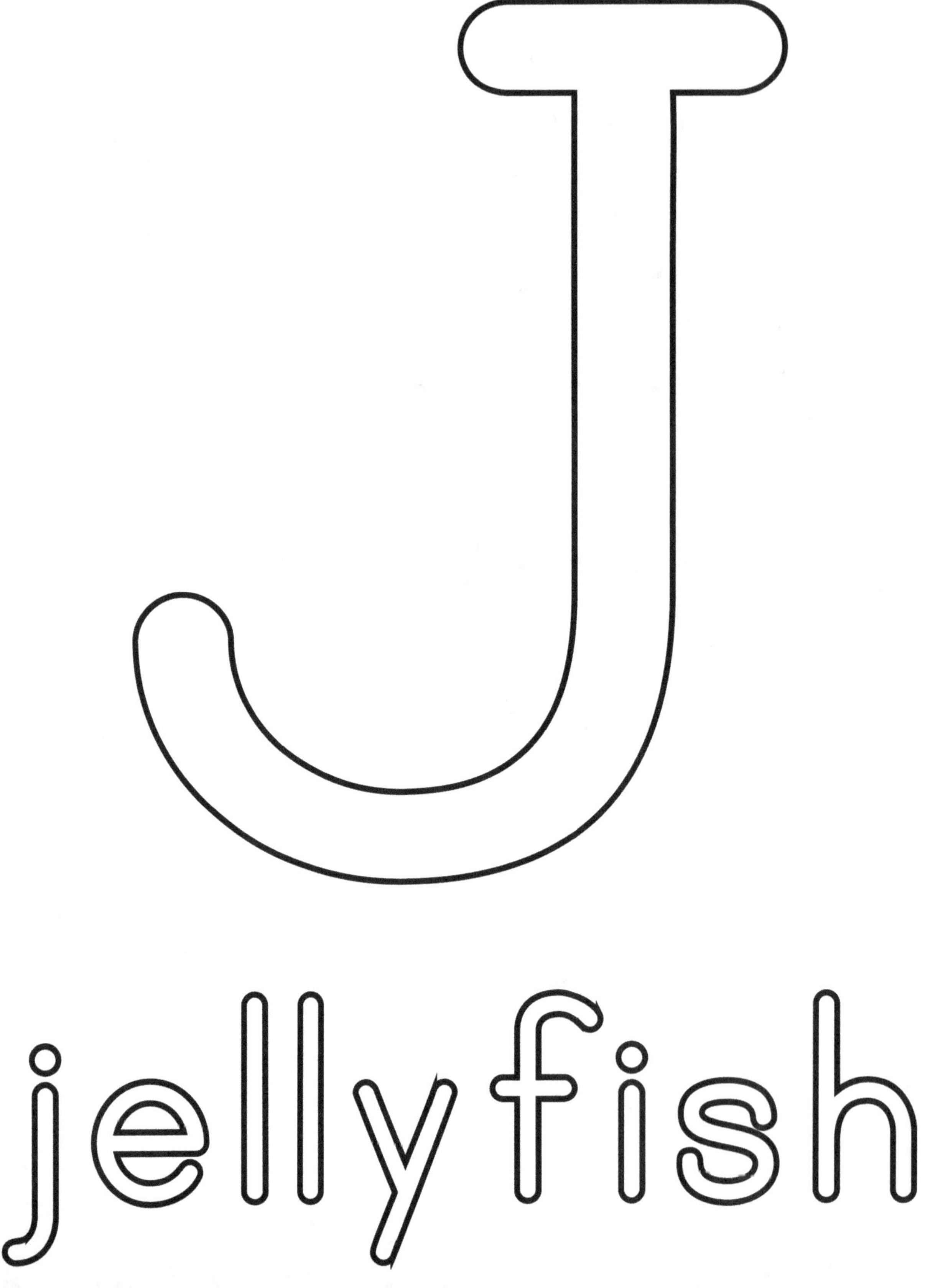

jellyfish

J

jellyfish

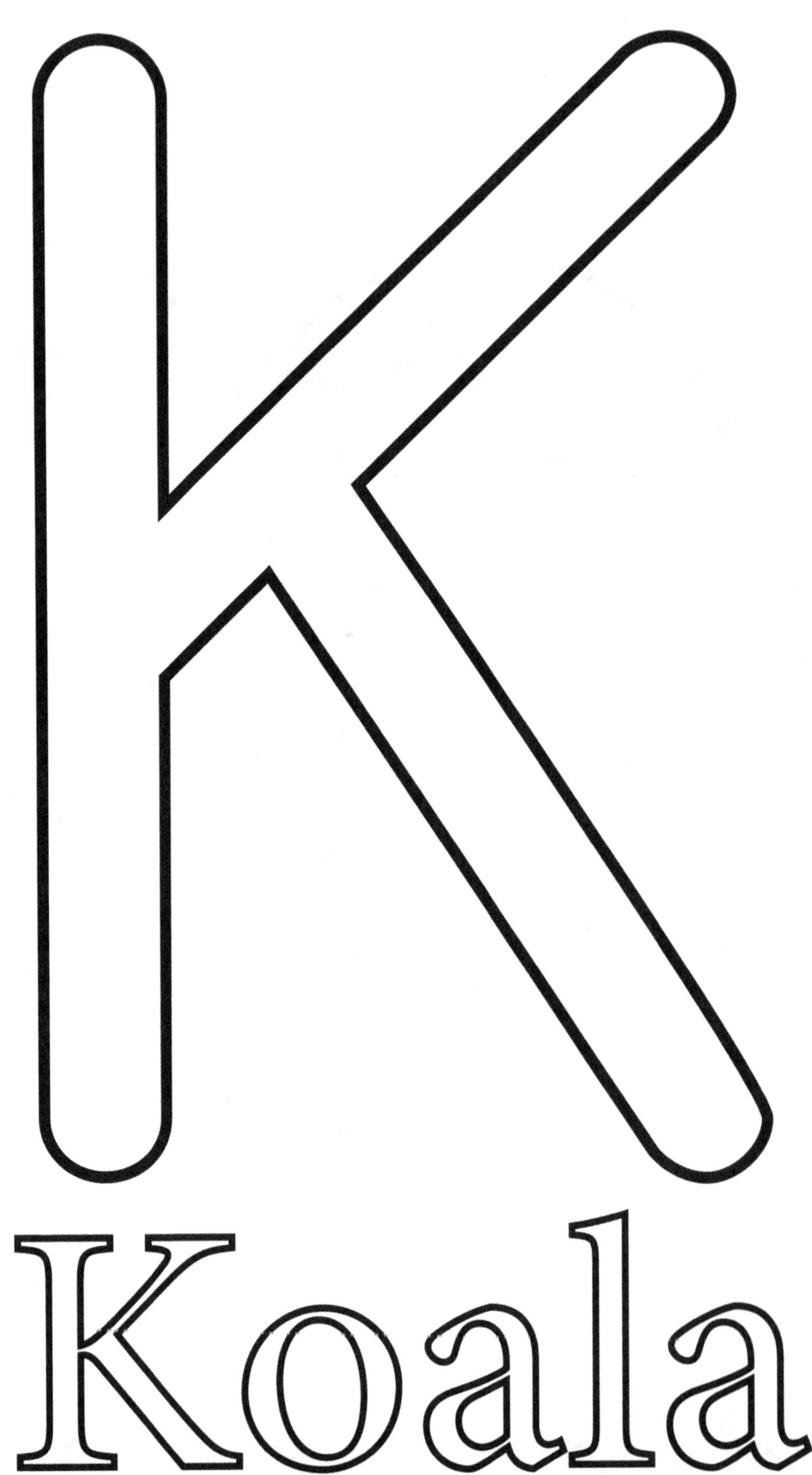

Koala

K

Koala

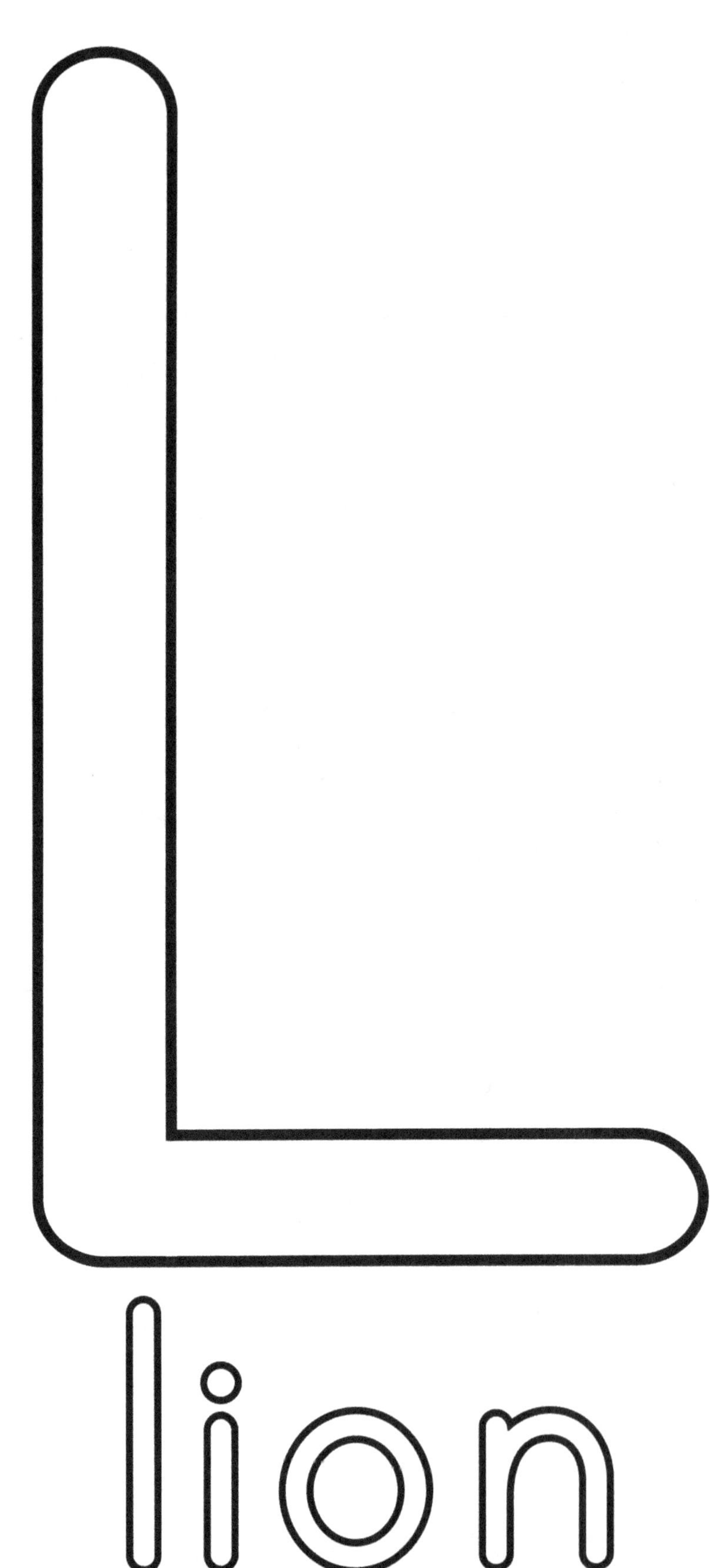

lion

Lion

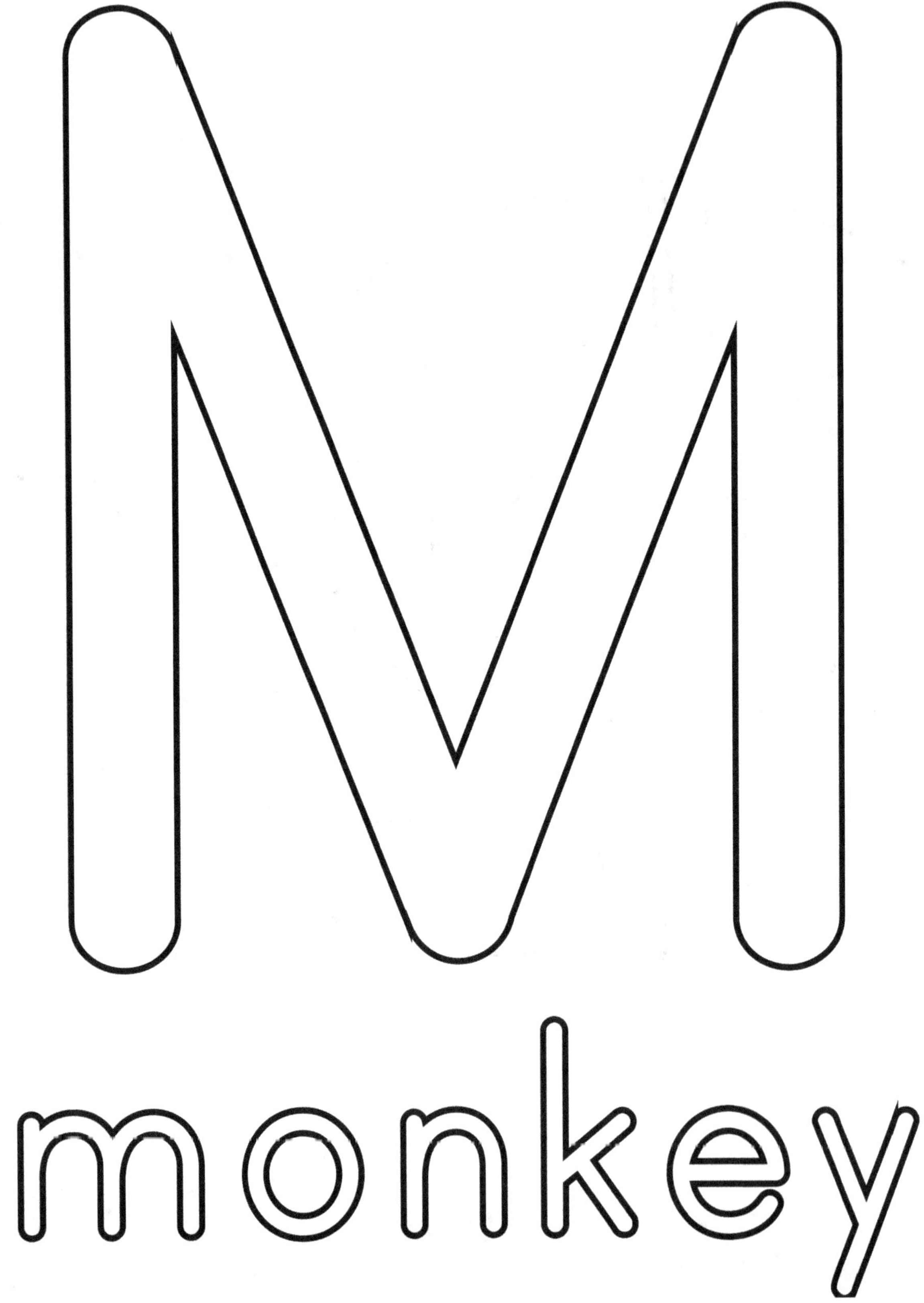

M
monkey

M

monkey

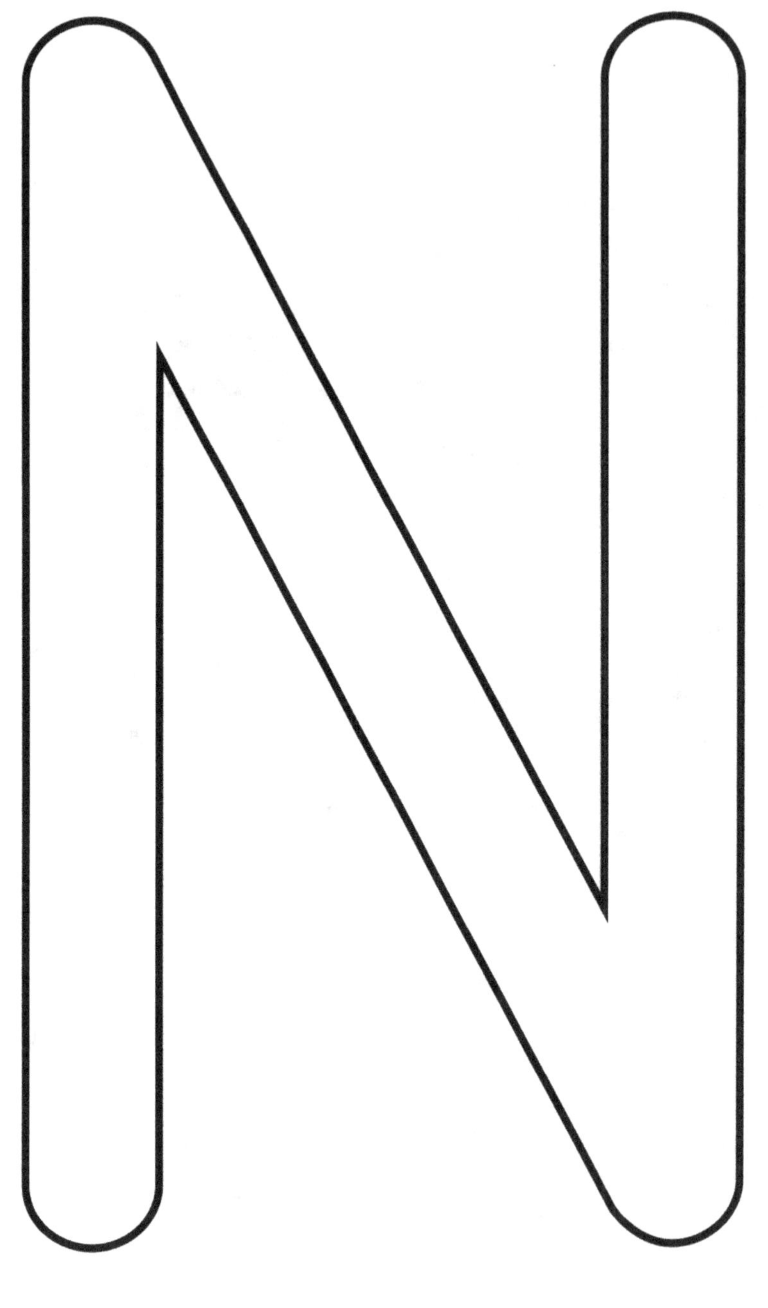

Narwhal

N

Narwhal

quail

quail

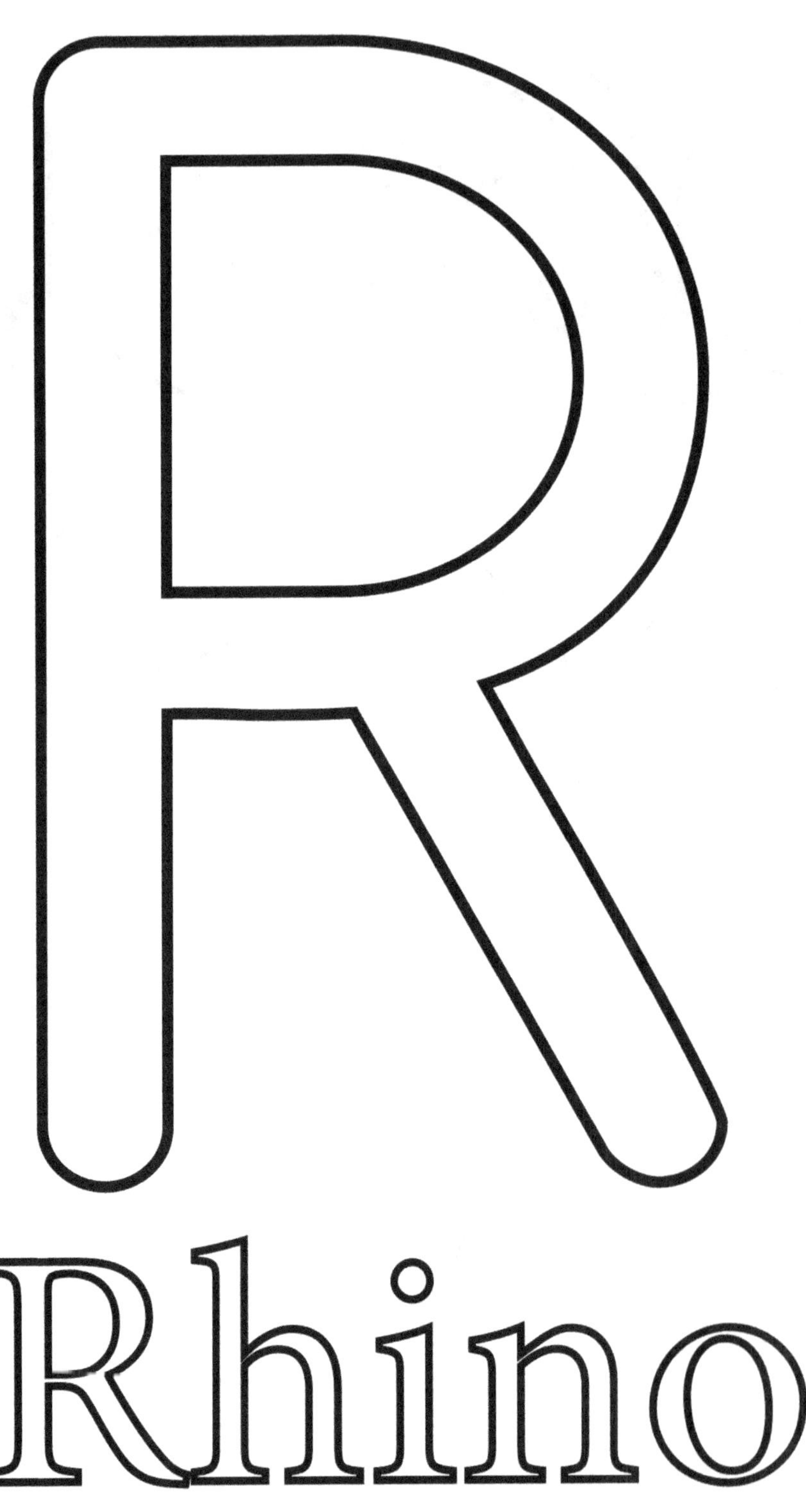

Rhino

R

RHINO

Squirrel

S

Squirrel

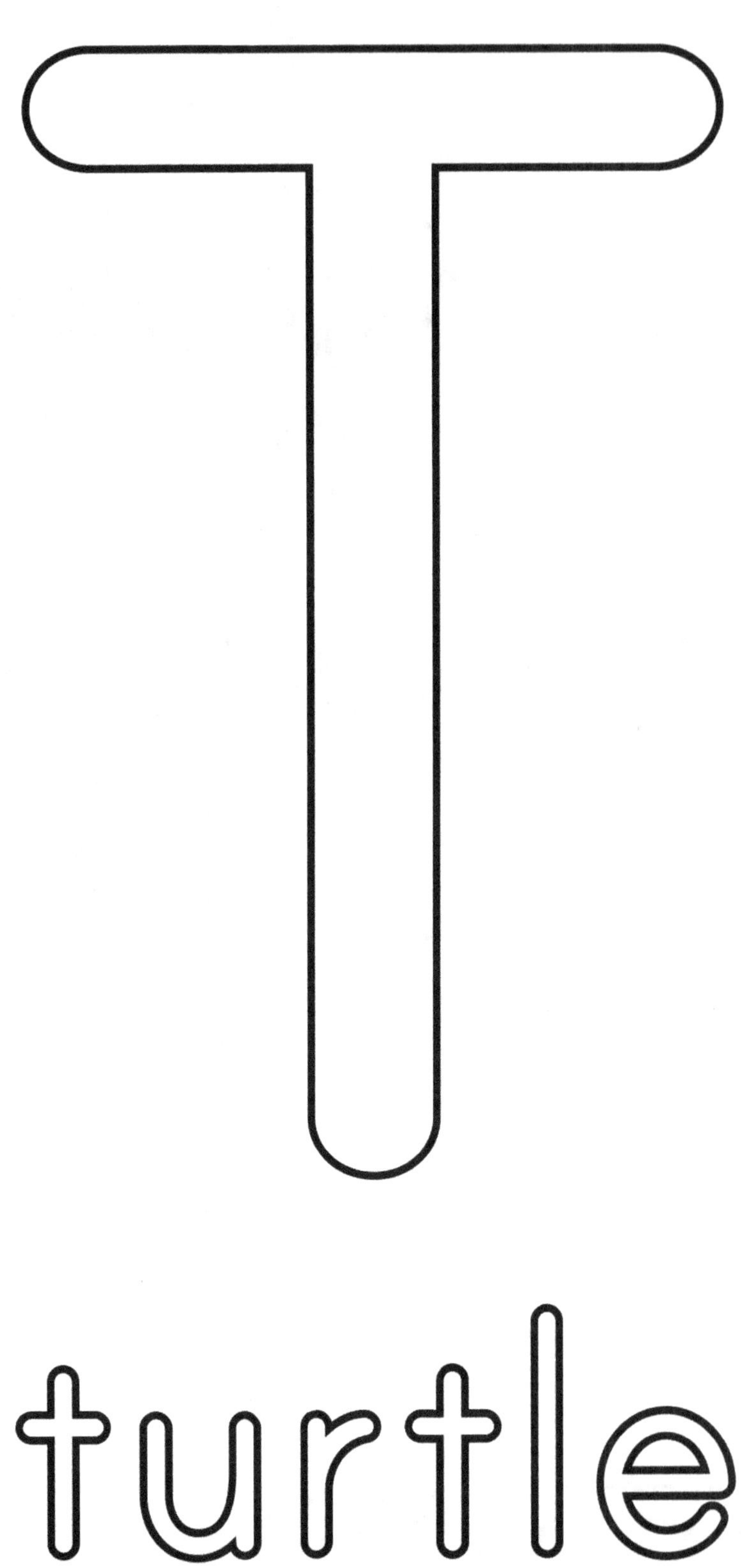

T
turtle

T turtle

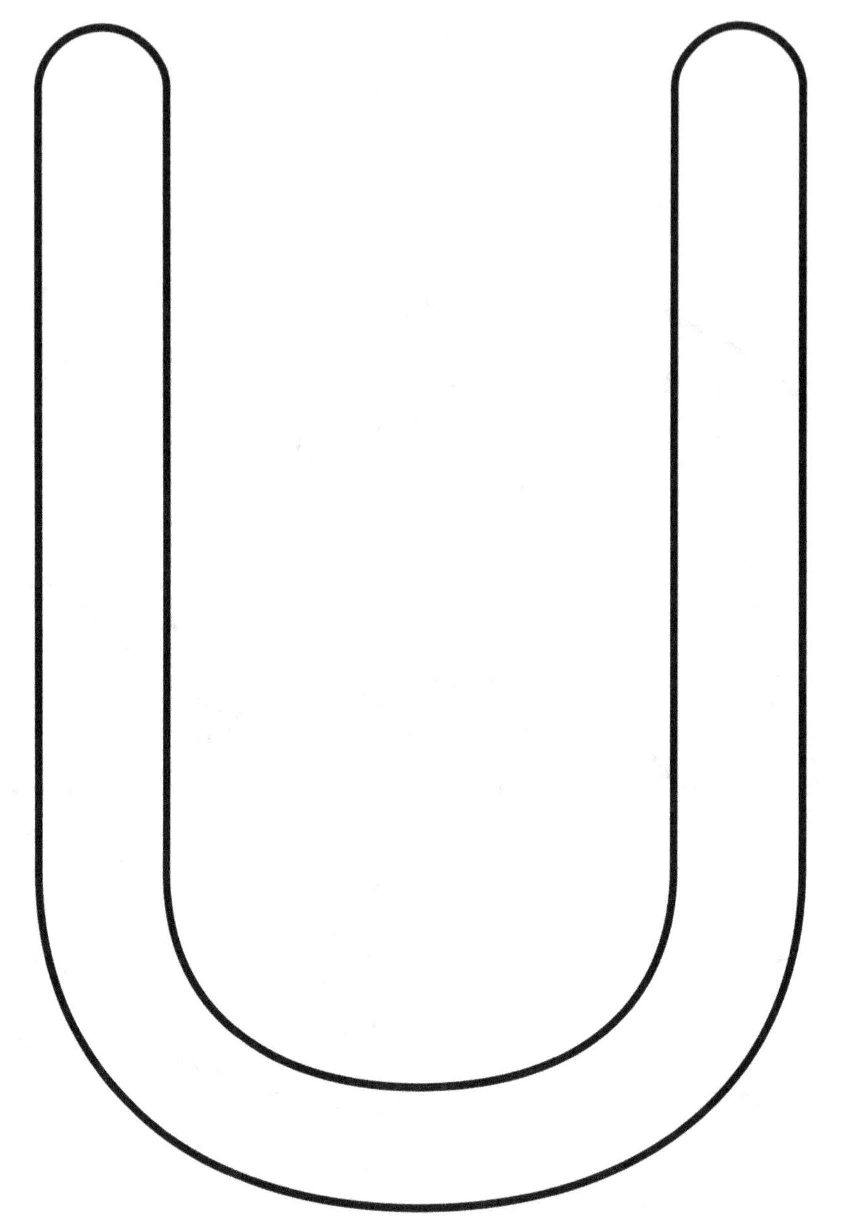

unicorn

U

Unicorn

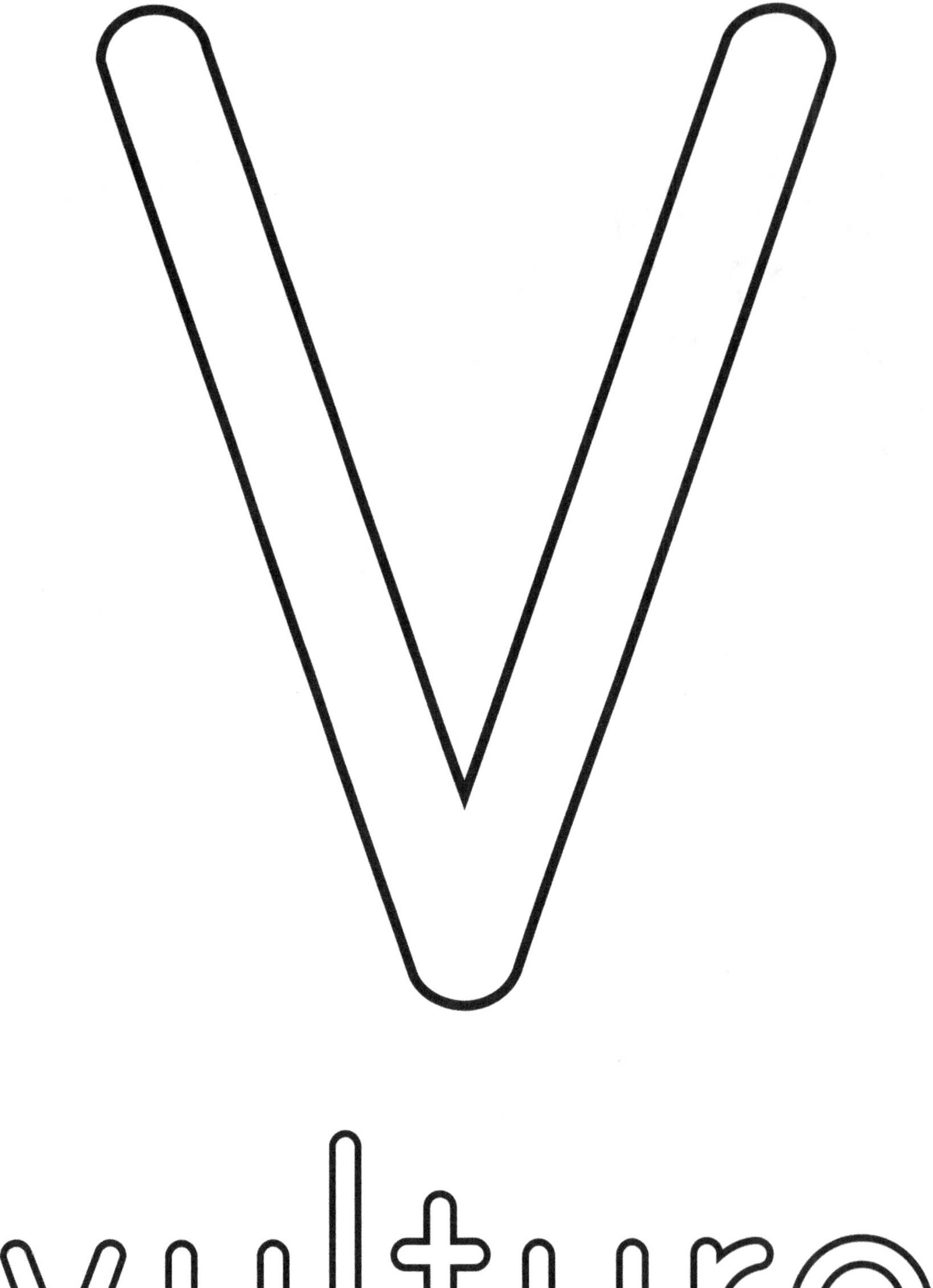

vulture

V

vulture

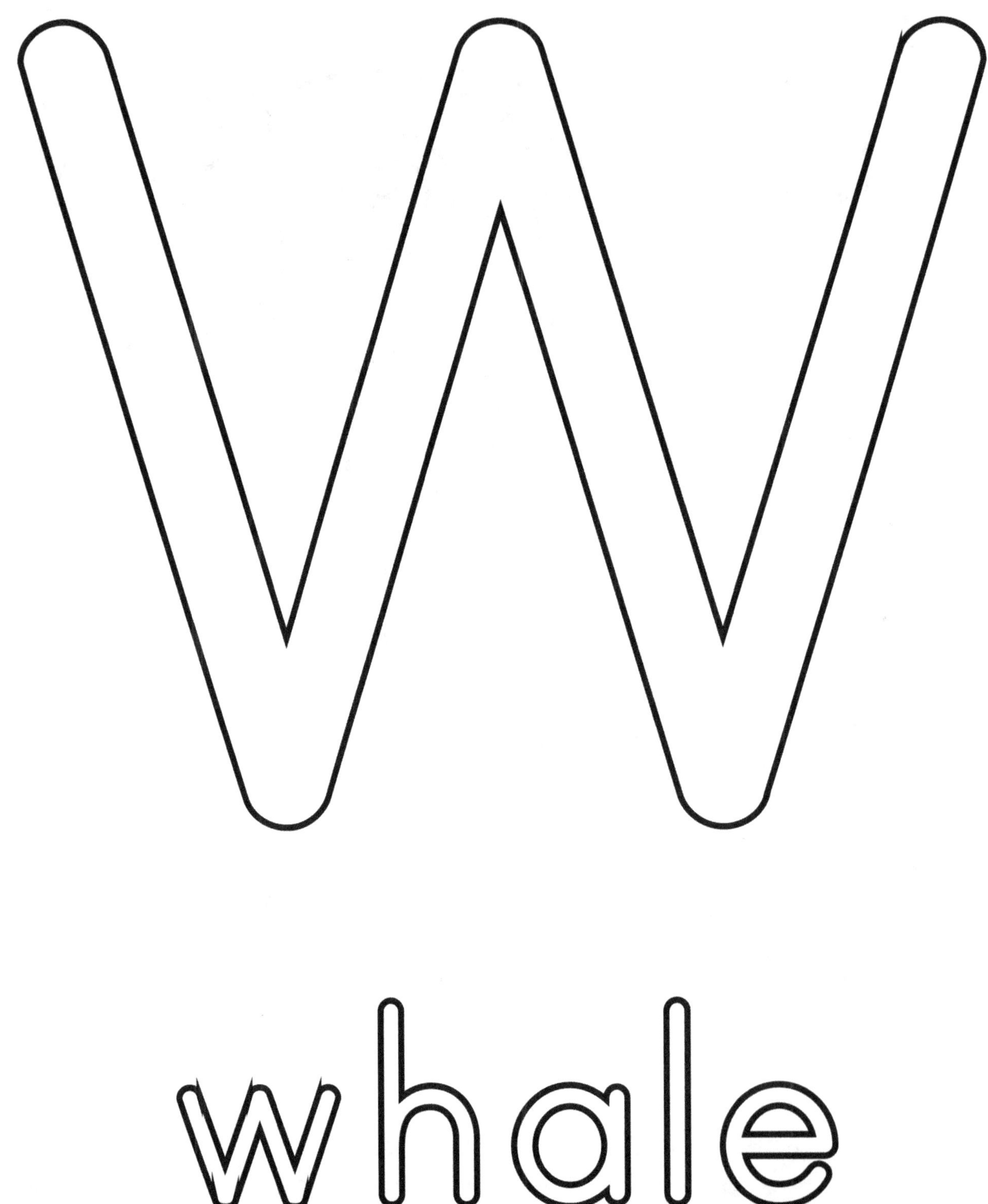

whale

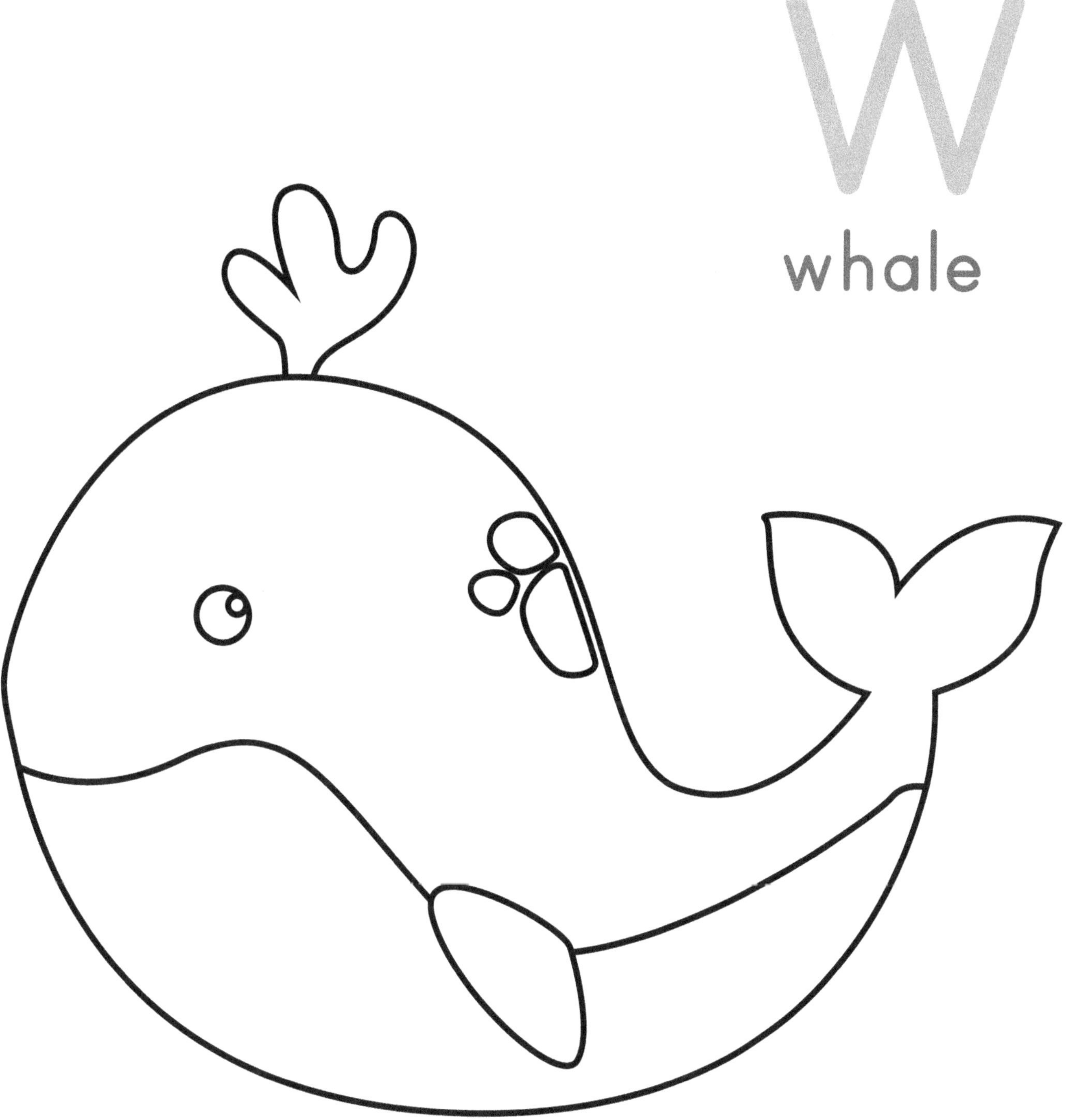

W

whale

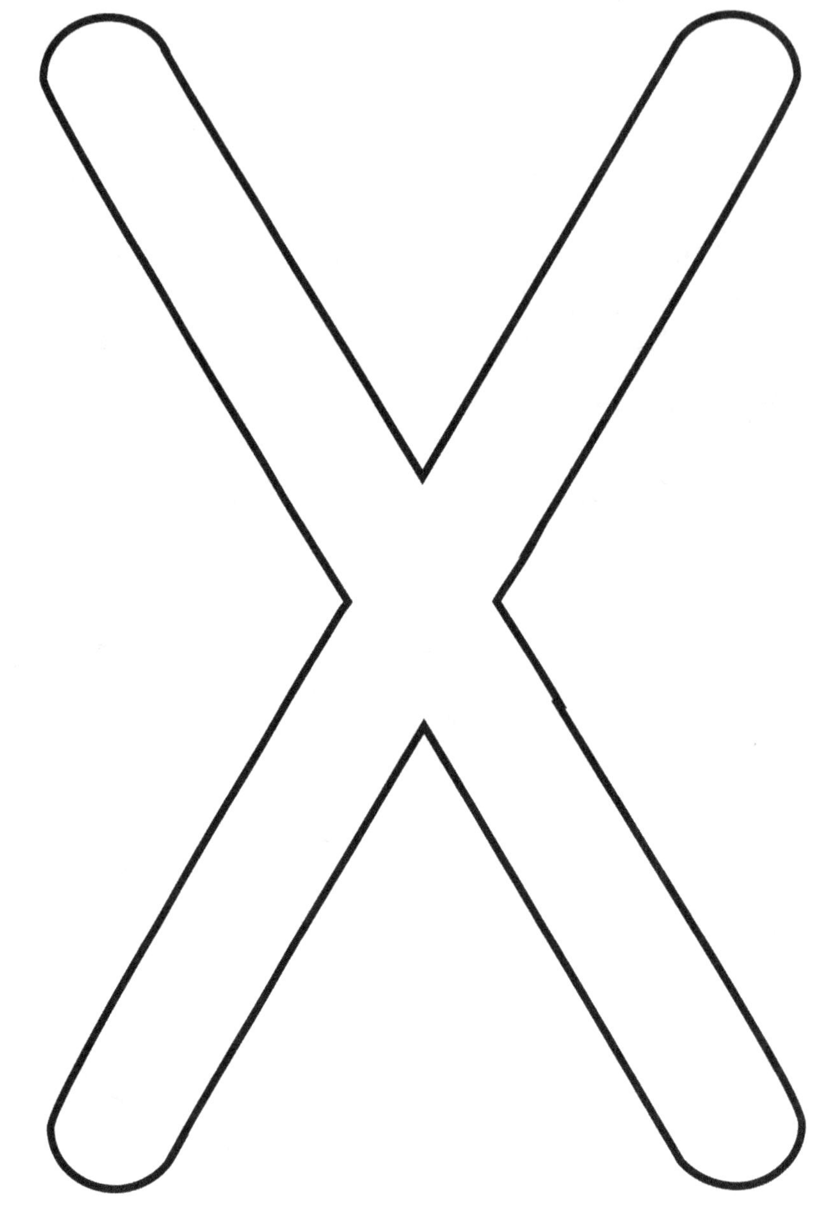

x-ray fish

X

x-ray fish

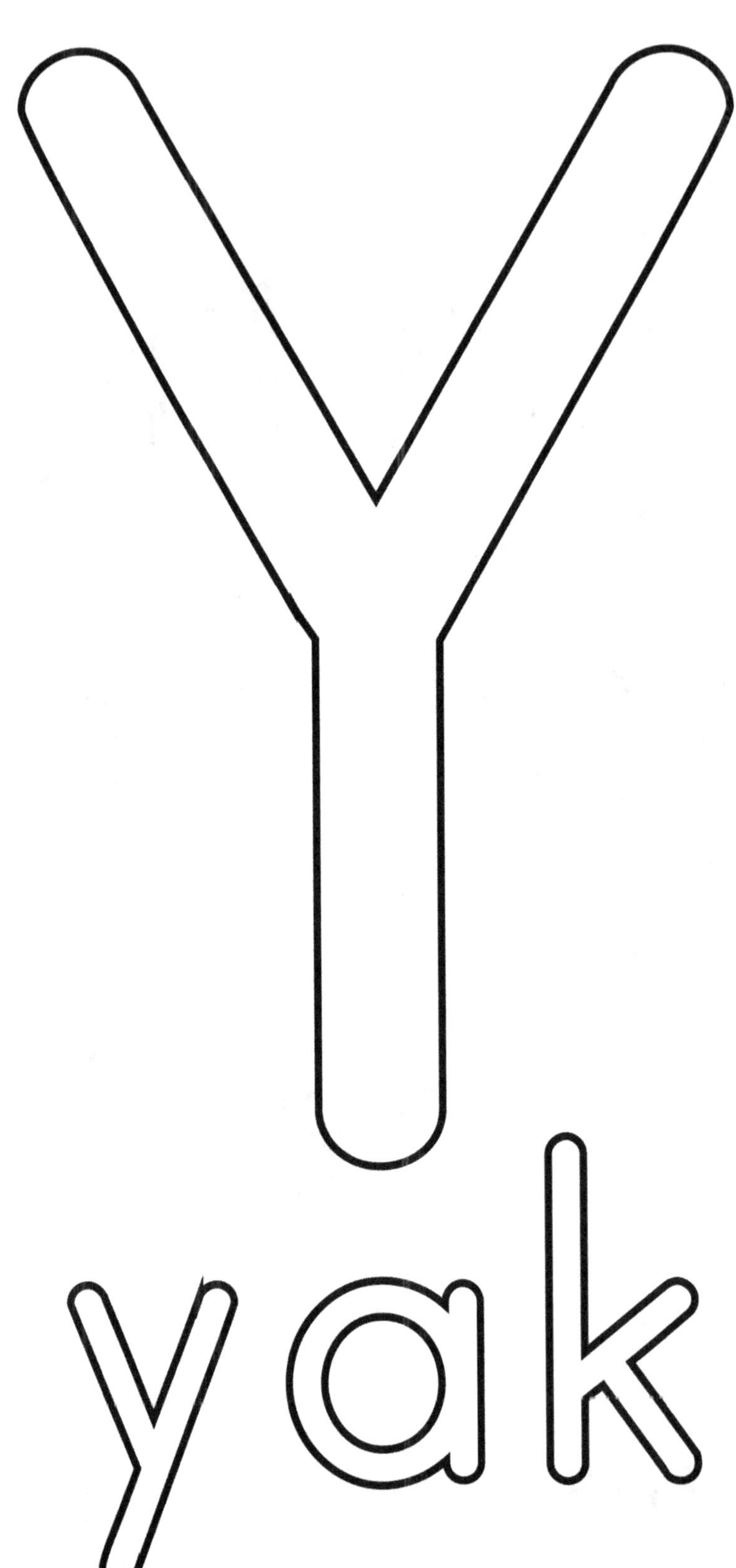

yak

Y

yak

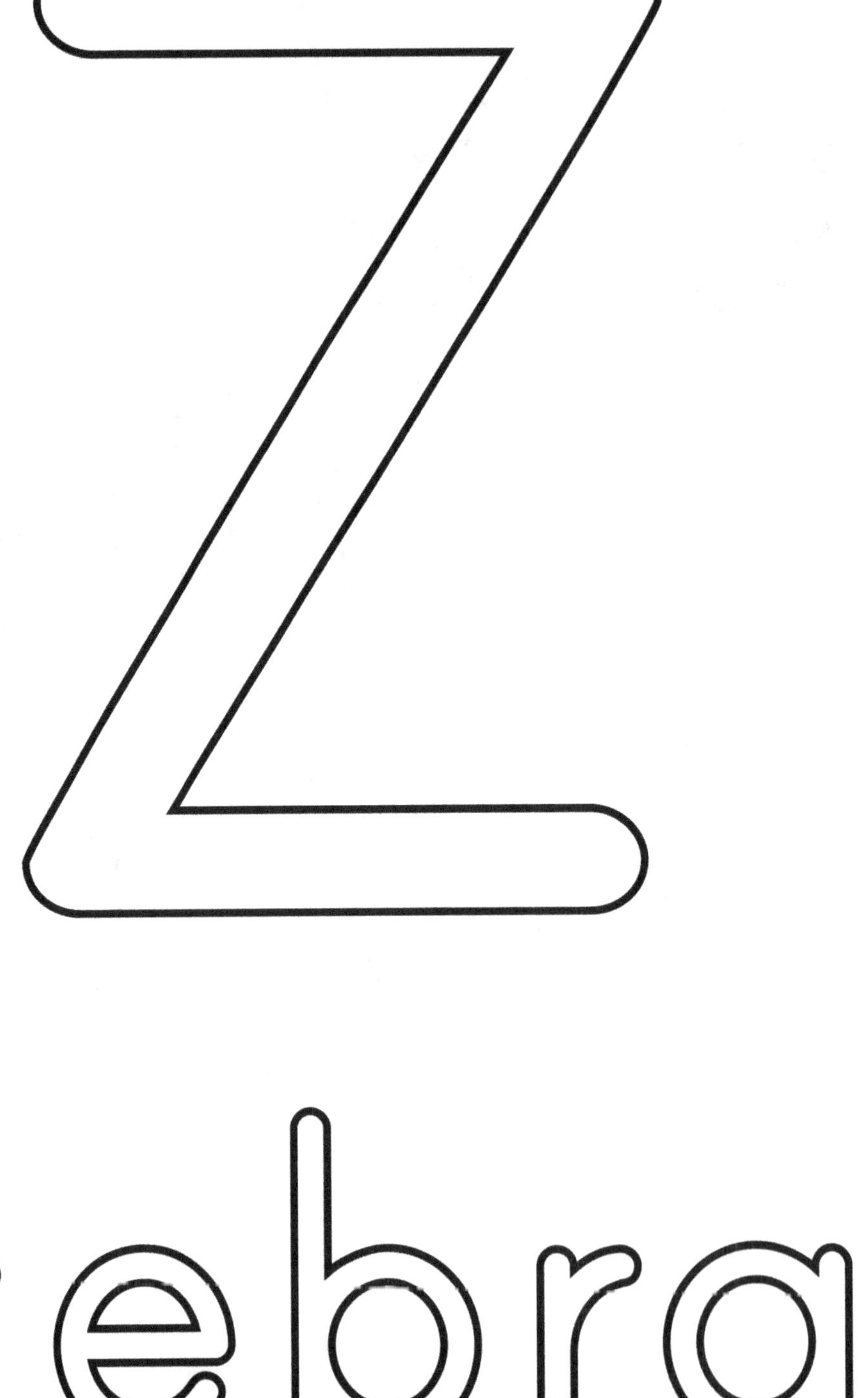

zebra

Z
zebra

1

square

red

2

rectangle

blue

circle

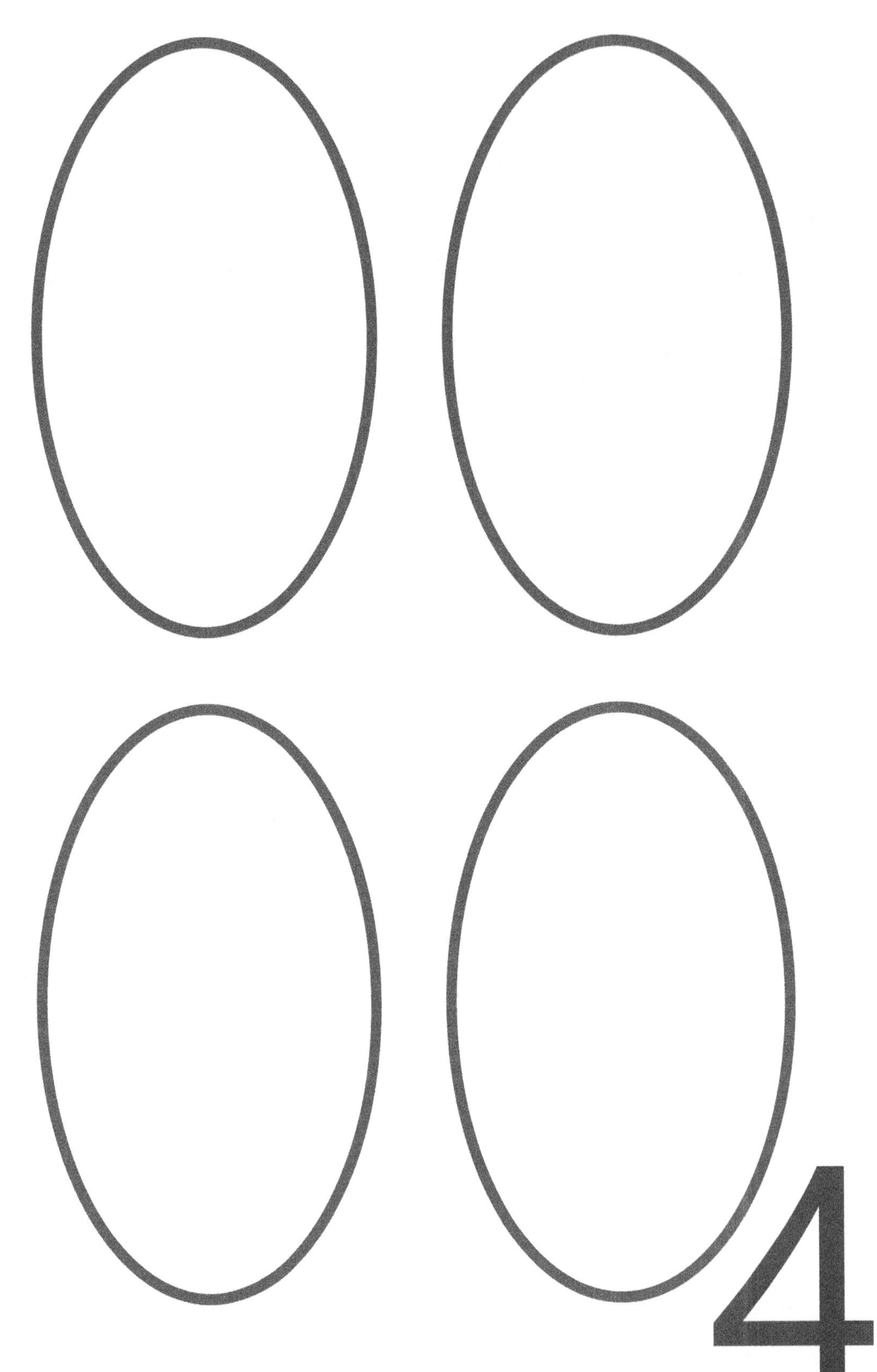

4

oval

brown

5

star

rhombus

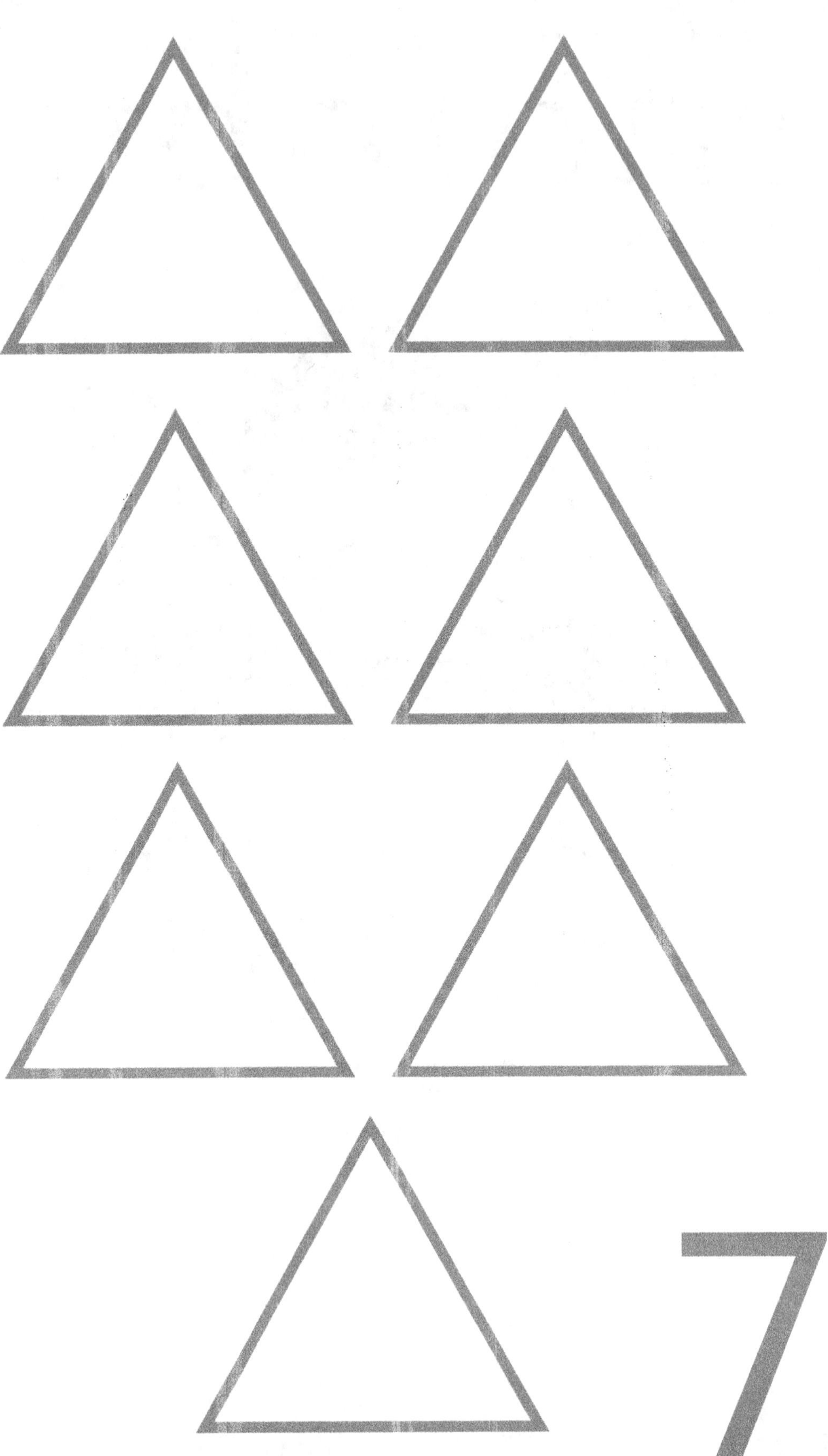
7

triangle

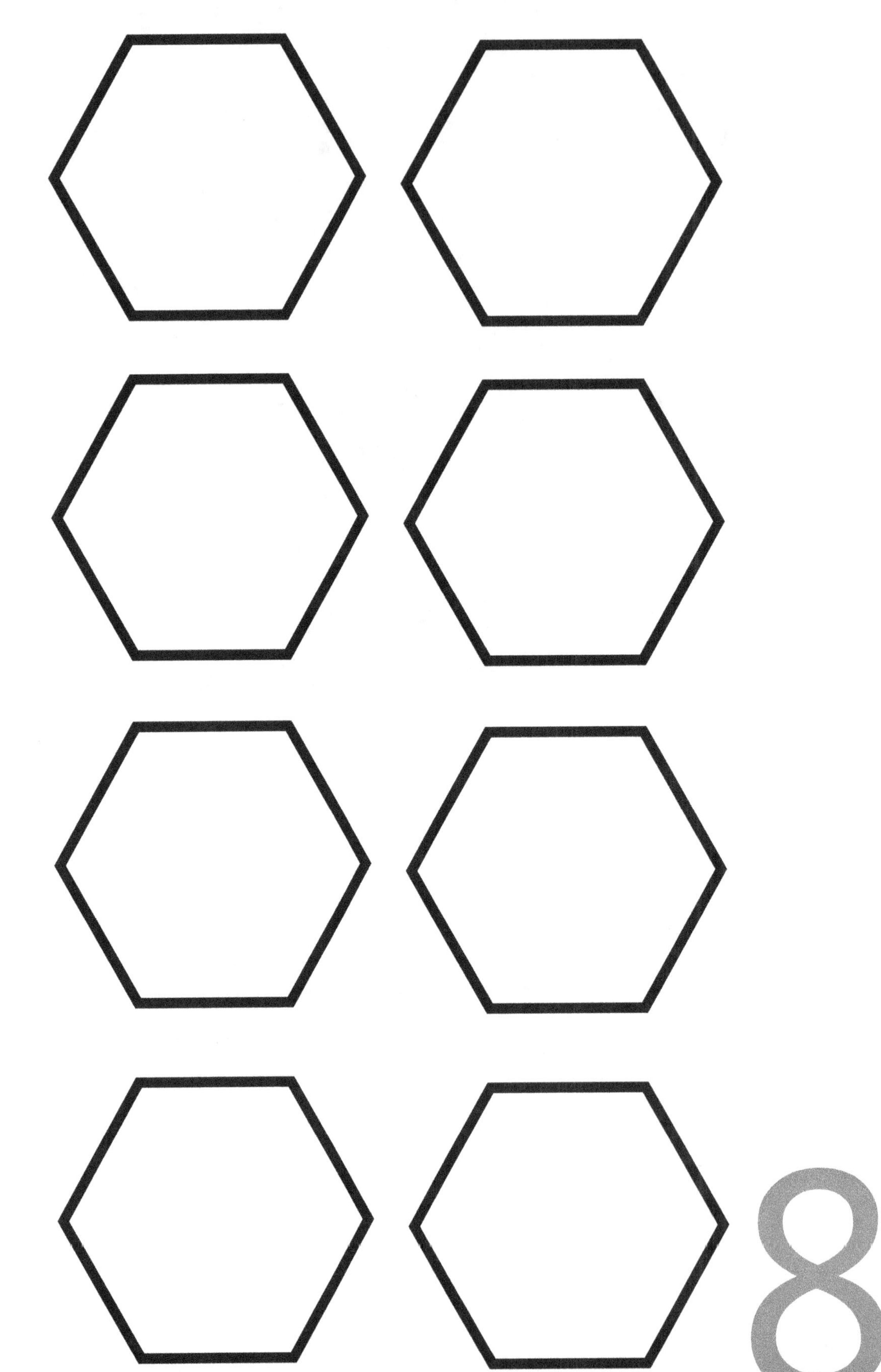

hexagon

black

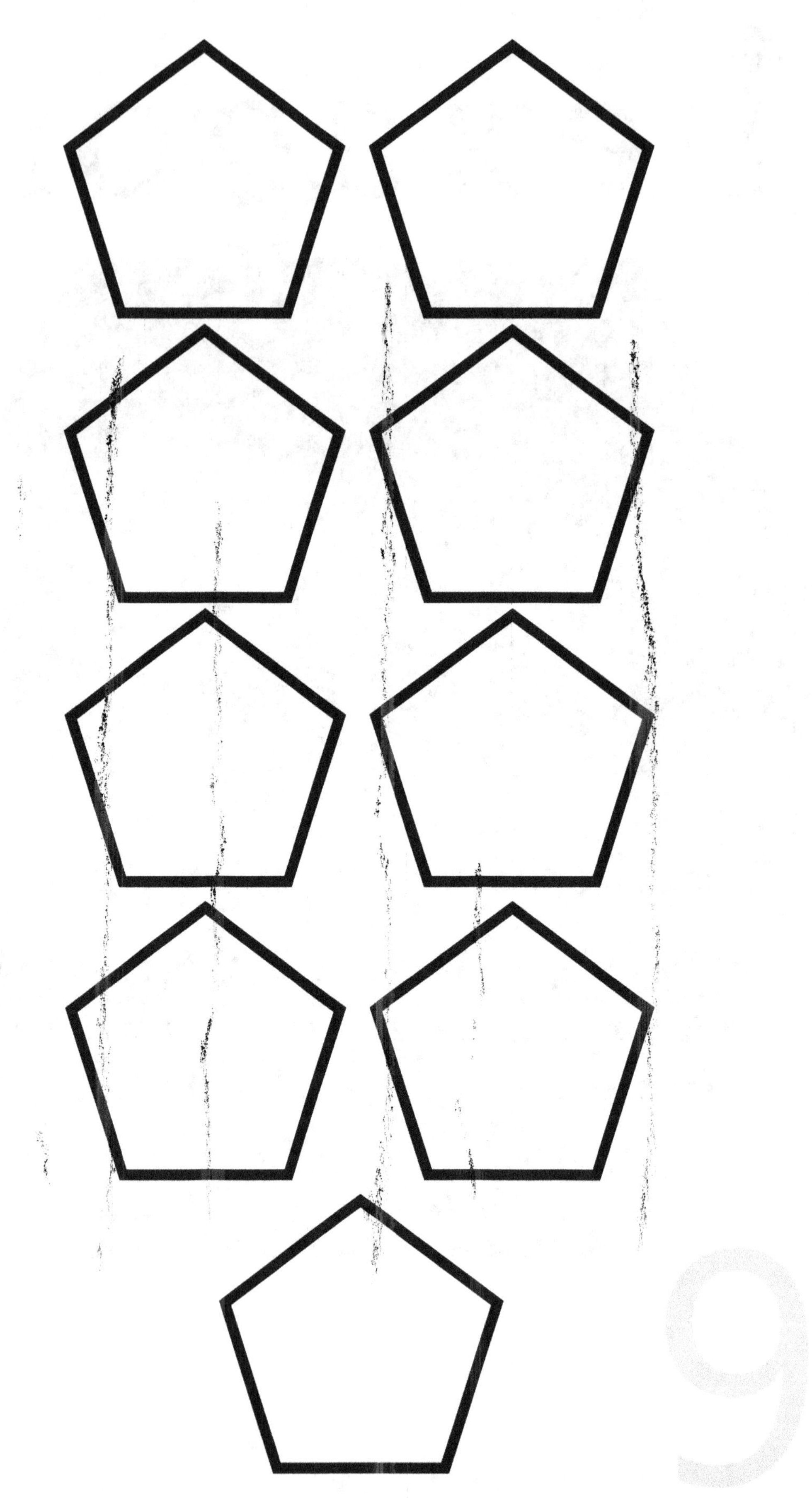

pentagon

10

heart